GW01454365

LOVREGLIC

Fantasia
on the Opera "La Traviata" by
Guiseppi Verdi

for clarinet and piano

Edited by

Colin Bradbury

CHESTER MUSIC

EDITOR'S NOTE

The nineteenth century saw an enthusiasm for Italian opera which live performance could never satisfy. In the absence of gramophone and radio the instrumental transcription flourished, and composers, often themselves virtuoso performers, found in the most popular arias ready material for their own sets of variations. Here is an outstanding example:

Donato Lovreglio (1841-1907) played the flute and composed many pieces for his own instrument, mainly operatic fantasias, as well as a few for the clarinet. He was born in Bari, but it seems that he spent most of his life in Naples. In *Fantasia on the Opera "La Traviata"* he demonstrates his remarkable ability to write variations, which, whilst providing a dazzling display of notes, nevertheless remain faithful to the character of the Verdi arias which inspired them.

Apart from the correction of obvious misprints, the addition of metronome marks and the resolution of discrepancies, the present version follows the original Ricordi edition of 1865.

Colin Bradbury

This piece has been recorded by
Colin Bradbury and Oliver Davies on ASV:ACM20 40

The *Fantasia on Airs from "I Puritani"* by Henry Lazarus
(1815-1895) is also included on this recording and sheet music is available
from Chester Music.

II
Fantasia
on the Opera
LA TRAVIATA
by Giuseppe Verdi

Al mio Amico
Nicola dell'Orefice

Donato Lovreglio
Op:45
Edited by Colin Bradbury

21
p dolciss.
pp 3
pp
30
p
p
pp
pp
39
pp
3
cresc. ed affrett.
f 3
rall.
pp 3
pp
cresc. ed affrett.
f
pp colla parte
47
mf con espressione e voce spiegata
pp
mf
3
mf
colla parte
pp
mf

52
57
riten.
colla parte
cresc.
pp secondando
riten.
63
marcate assai le note del canto e leggere le altre
p a tempo
69
fp

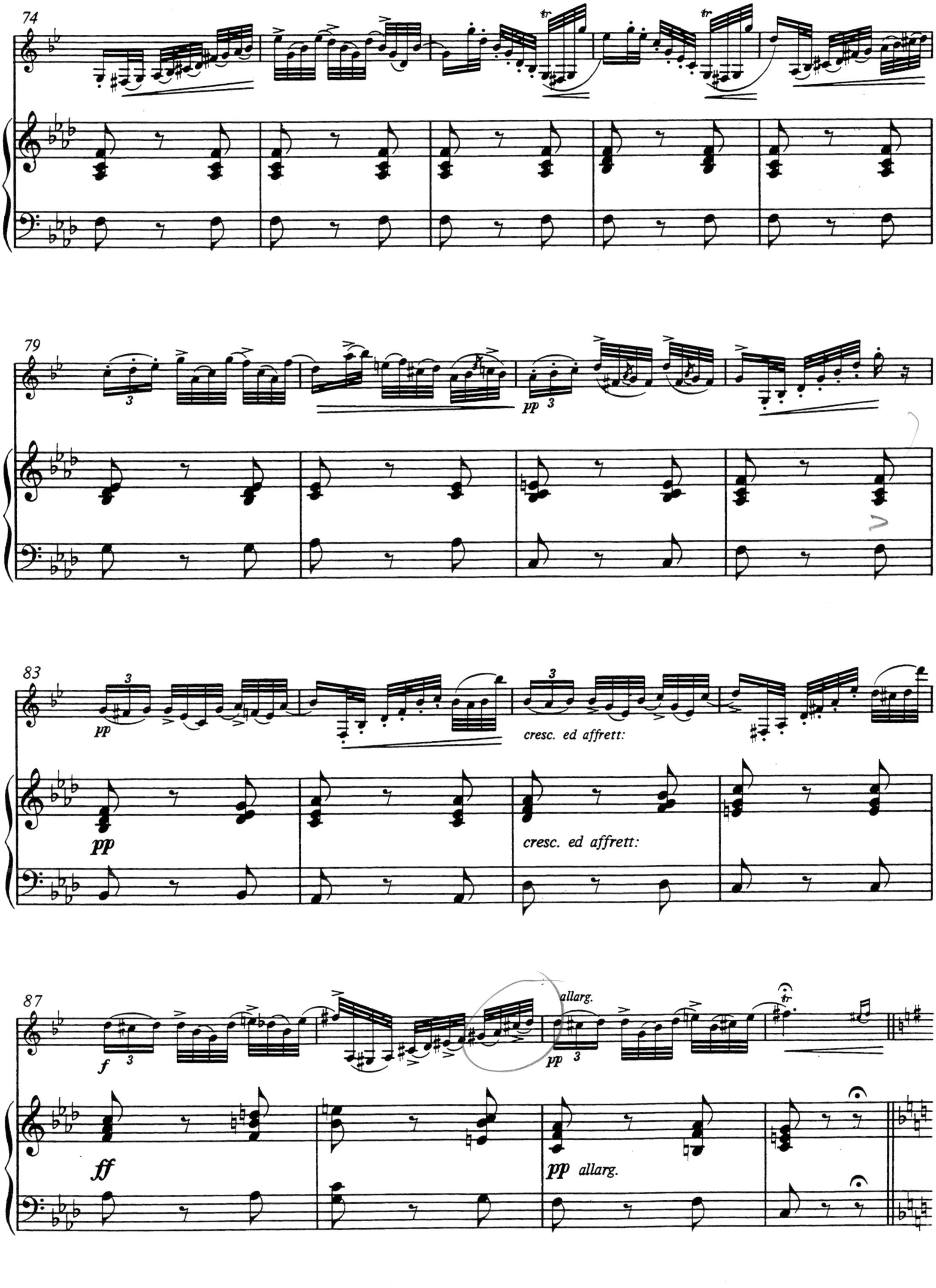
74
79
pp
83
pp
cresc. ed affrett:
87
f
ff
allarg.
pp allarg.

91
voce piena
expansive
94
97
rit.
a tempo
colla parte
rit.
a tempo
100
legg.
riten.
a tempo
cresc.
riten.
a tempo
cresc.

103
rall.
a tempo
riten.
a tempo
riten.
legg.
pp rall.
a tempo
riten.
a tempo
riten.
106
a tempo
riten.
a tempo
riten.
conforza
a tempo
p riten.
a tempo
p riten.
109
110
cresc. ed affrett.
Allegro [♩. =108]
p affrett.
sempre
ff

120
ff
126
Meno assai [♩. =69]
8va
ppp
ppp
132
p
p
poco rit.
poco rit.
138
Poco più mosso
p
f
p

142
Più mosso
meno
p
rall.
ff
stent.
meno p
rall.
Allegretto Scherzando [♩. =69]
148
p
tr
152
f p
f pp
tr
156
f
f pp

160
p
f
164
cresc.
f
pp
cresc.
cresc.
168
Più mosso
f
pp
ff
172
Andante con espressione [♩ =69]
pp
ppp
stent. assai
molto legato
Ped

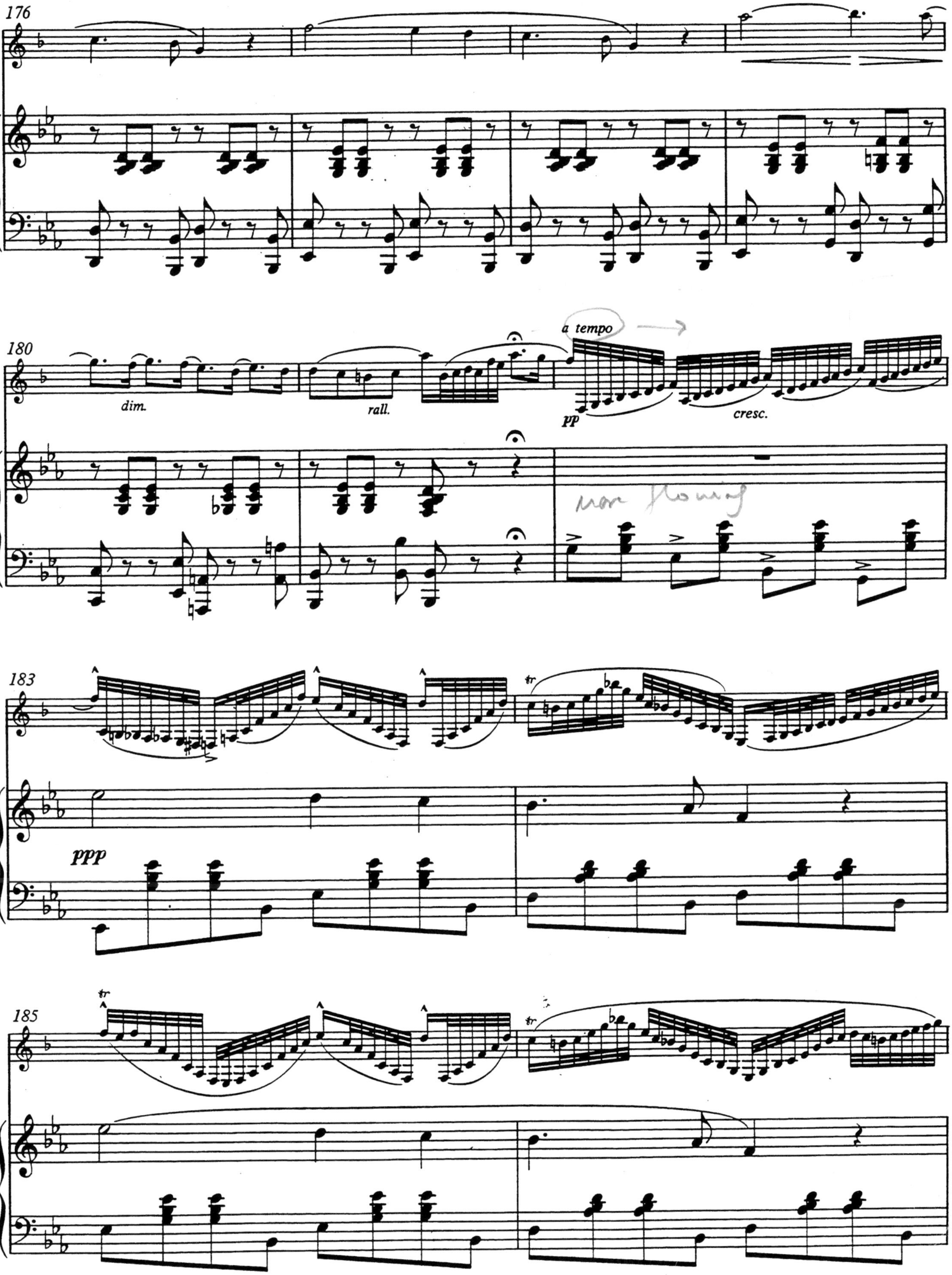
176
180
dim.
rall.
a tempo
pp
cresc.
183
ppp
tr
185
tr
tr

187
f
p
pp
189
190
tr
cresc.
ff
lento
191
p dim.
pp
ppp
cresc. ed affrett.
al
Allegro brillante
ff
marc.

196
Poco meno mosso
ritenuto assai
Allegro [♩. =88]
p
pp
ritenuto assai
ppp
ff
202
pp
207
p
p
213
cresc.
ff
ff

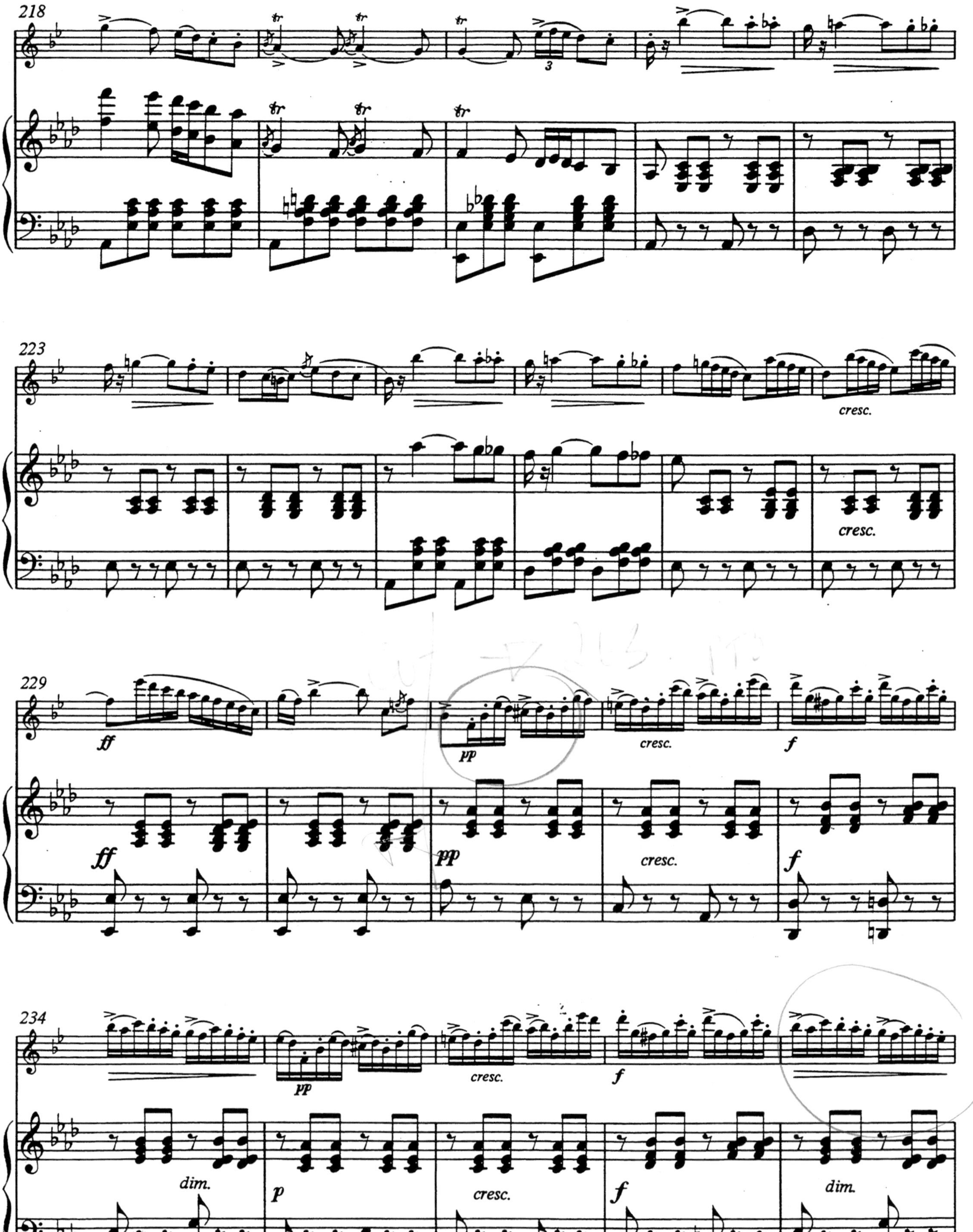
218
tr
223
cresc.
229
ff
pp
cresc.
f
234
dim.
pp
p
cresc.
f
dim.

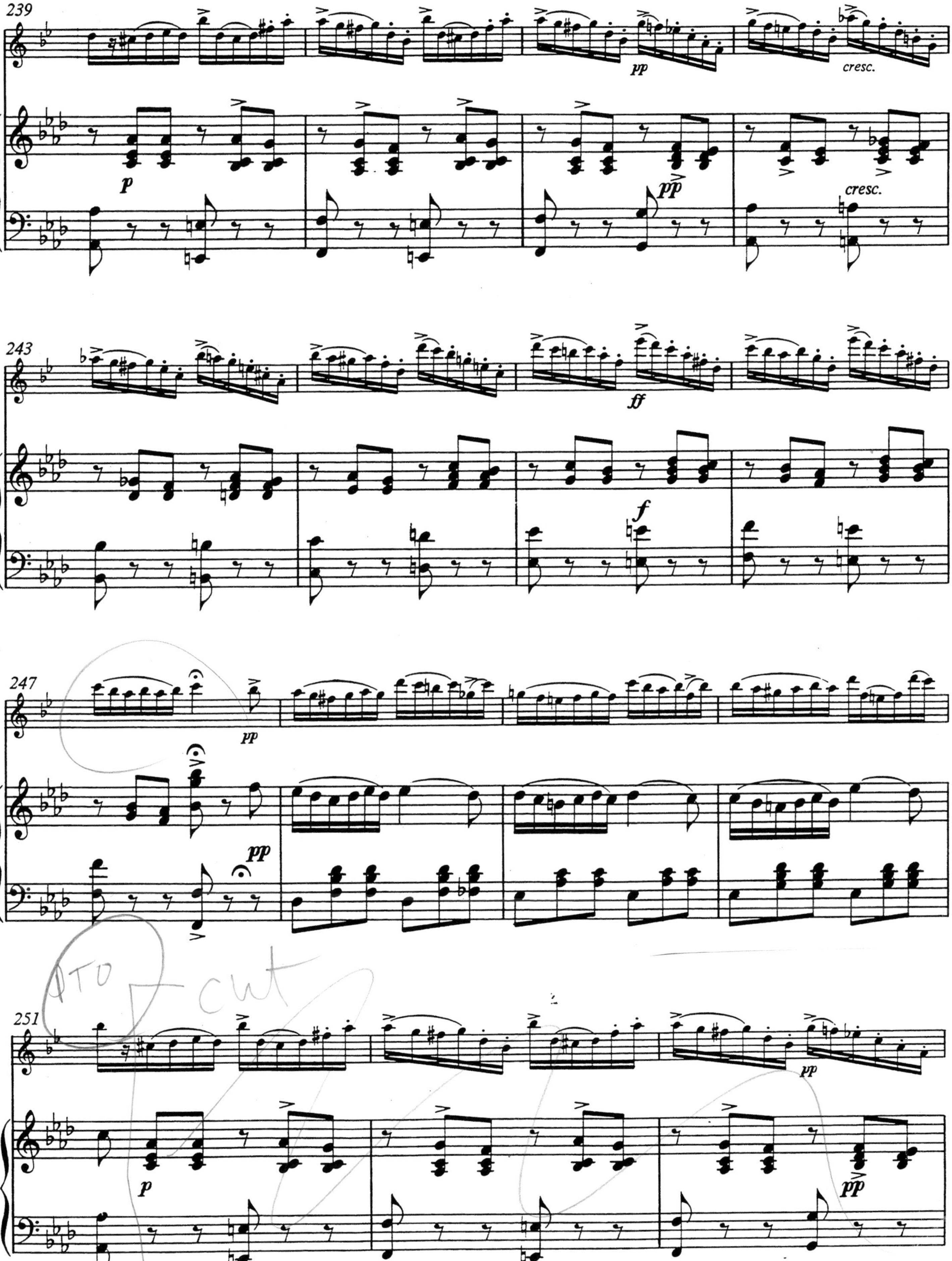
239
pp
cresc.
p
pp
cresc.
243
ff
f
247
pp
pp
251
cut
p
pp
pp

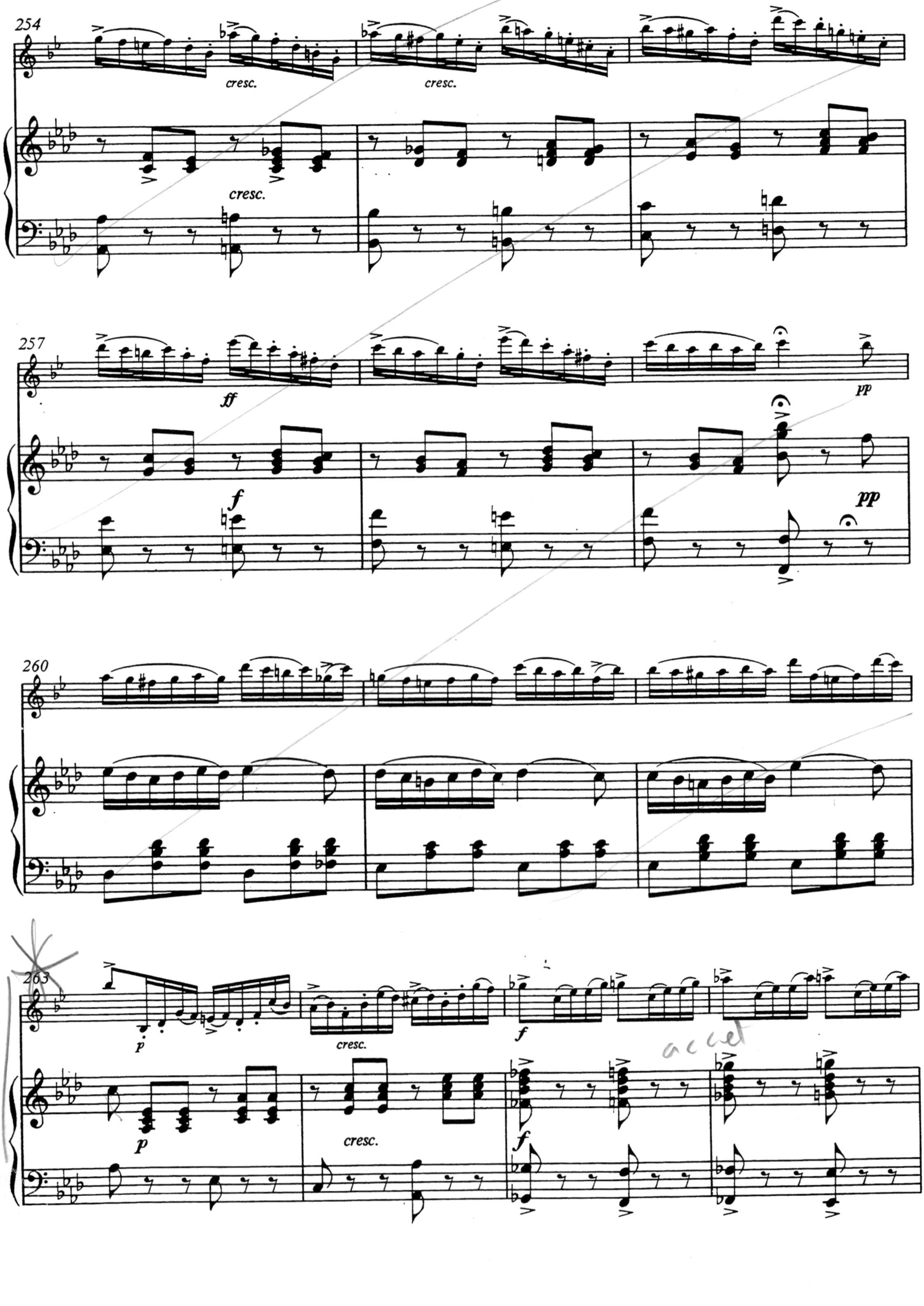
254
cresc.
cresc.
cresc.
257
ff
f
pp
pp
260
263
p
p
cresc.
cresc.
f
f

Printed and bound in the United Kingdom by Staples Printers Rochester Limited

1/97 (26887)

SELECTED MUSIC FOR CLARINET AND PIANO

BÄCK	Elegy
BAKER	Cantilena
BOYLE	Sonatina
DEBUSSY	Première Rhapsodie
DEBUSSY	Two Pieces
FALLA	Two Pieces from *El Amor Brujo*
GADE	Fantasy Pieces Op. 43
HOROWITZ	Concertino for Clarinet and Strings
KALLIWODA	Morceau de Salon Op. 299
LUTOSLAWSKI	Dance Preludes
MACONCHY	Fantasia for Clarinet and Piano
MOZART	Divertimento No 1 (from K439b)
MOZART	Divertimento No 2 (from K439b)
MOZART	Divertimento No 3 (from K439b)
OBERTHUR	Le Désir
POULENC	Sonata
SAINT-SAËNS	Sonata
SZALOWSKI	Sonatina
STANFORD	Three Intermezzi
WATERSON	Morceau de Concert
WOOD	Paraphrase

SOLO CLARINET

BENTZON	Theme and Variations Op. 14
BERKELEY	Three Pieces
MORTENSEN	Sonatina Op. 9
STRAVINSKY	Three Pieces

From

CHESTER MUSIC